SSF

Talking Hands

FEELINGS AND EMOTIONS

SENTIMIENTOS

WRITTEN BY KATHLEEN PETELINSEK AND E. RUSSELL PRIMM
ILLUSTRATED BY KATIE OPSETH

A SPECIAL THANKS TO OUR ADVISERS: AS A MEMBER OF A DEAF FAMILY THAT SPANS FOUR
GENERATIONS, KIM BIANCO MAJERI LIVES, WORKS, AND PLAYS AMONGST THE DEAF COMMUNITY.

CARMINE L. VOZZOLO IS AN EDUCATOR OF CHILDREN WHO ARE
DEAF AND HARD OF HEARING, AS WELL AS THEIR FAMILIES.

The Child's World®

Published in the United States of America by The Child's World®
PO Box 326, Chanhassen, MN 55317-0326
800-599-READ
www.childsworld.com

Photo Credits: All photographs copyright © Rubber Ball Productions

The Child's World®: Mary Berendes, Publishing Director

Editorial Directions, Inc.: E. Russell Primm, Editorial Director; Katie Marsico and Elizabeth K. Martin, Associate Editors; Kathleen Petelinsek and E. Russell Primm, Photo Researchers

The Design Lab: Kathleen Petelinsek, design, and page production; Kari Thornborough, production assistant

LIBRARY OF CONGRESS CATALOGING-IN-PUBLICATION DATA
Petelinsek, Kathleen.
    Feelings and emotions = Sentimientos / by Kathleen Petelinsek and E. Russell Primm ; content advisers, Carmine L. Vozzolo and Kim Bianco Majeri.
       p. cm. — (Talking hands)
    Summary: Provides illustrations of American Sign Language signs and Spanish and English text for various feelings.
    English, Spanish, and American Sign Language.
    ISBN 1-59296-022-7 (lib. bdg. : alk. paper) 1. American Sign Language—Vocabulary—Juvenile literature. 2. Spanish language—Vocabulary—Juvenile literature. 3. Emotions—Juvenile literature. [1. American Sign Language—Vocabulary. 2. Spanish language—Vocabulary. 3. Polyglot materials. 4. Emotions.] I. Title: Sentimientos. II. Primm, E. Russell, 1958– III. Title.
    HV2476.P474 2004
    419'.7—dc22   2003018692

NOTE TO PARENTS AND EDUCATORS:

The understanding of any language begins with the acquisition of vocabulary, whether the language is spoken or manual. The books in the Talking Hands series provide readers, both young and old, with a first introduction to basic American Sign Language signs. Combining close photo cues and simple, but detailed, line illustration, children and adults alike can begin the process of learning American Sign Language. In addition to the English word and sign for that word, we have included the Spanish word. The addition of the Spanish word is a wonderful way to allow children to see multiple ways (English, Spanish, signed) to say the same word. This is also beneficial for Spanish-speaking families to learn the sign even though they may not know the English word for that object.

Let these books be an introduction to the world of American Sign Language. Most languages have regional dialects and multiple ways of expressing the same thought. This is also true for sign language. We have attempted to use the most common version of the signs for the words in this series. As with any language, the best way to learn is to be taught in person by a frequent user. It is our hope that this series will pique your interest in sign language.

Amazed
Asombrado

1.

2.

3.

3

Angry
Enfadado

1.

2.

Cranky
Malhumorado

1.

2.

Repeat
Repita

Defiant
Atrevido

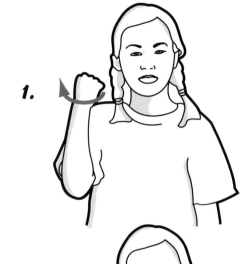

1.

2.

6

Disappointed
Desilusionado

1.

2.

Disgusted
Indignado

1.

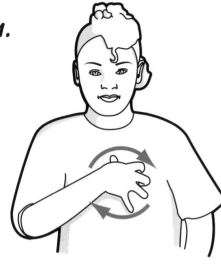

Doubtful
Incierto

1.

2.

Repeat
Repita

Frustrated
Frustrado

1.

2.

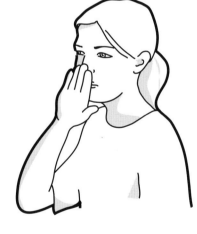

Happy
Feliz

1.

Repeat
Repita

11

Hurt
Herido

1.

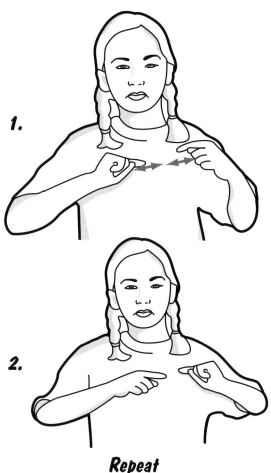

2.

Repeat
Repita

Proud
Orgulloso

1.

2.

Puzzled
Perplejo

1.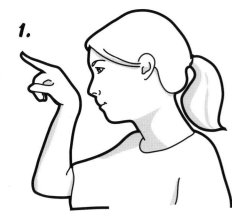

2.

Sad
Triste

1.

2.

Satisfied
Satisfecho

1.

2.
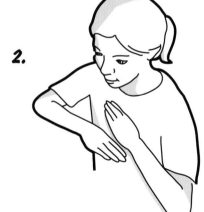

Selfish
Egoísta

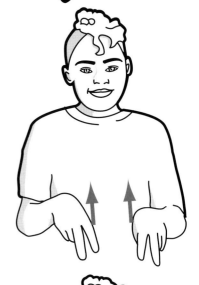

1.

2.

Shy
Tímido

1.

2.

Sorry
Arrepentido

1.

2.

Thoughtful
Pensativo

1.

Repeat
Repita

20

Thrilled
Contentísimo

1.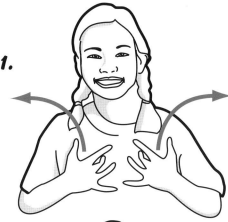

2.

Upset
Alterado

1.

2.

Worried
Preocupado

1.

2.

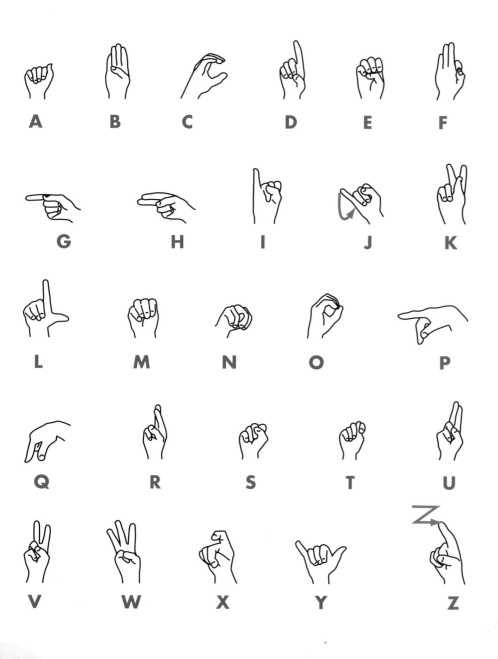

A B C D E F

G H I J K

L M N O P

Q R S T U

V W X Y Z

A SPECIAL THANK-YOU

to our models from the Program for Childr
Who Are Deaf and Hard of Hearing at th
Alexander Graham Bell Elementary Schoo
in Chicago, Illinois:

Aroosa is in third grade in Milwaukee and loves reading, shopping, and playing with he sister Aamna. Aroosa's favorit color is red.

Carla is in fourth grade and enjoys art, as well as all kinds of sports.

Deandre likes playing football and watching NFL games on television. He also looks forwa to going to the movies with his family.

Destiny enjoys music and dancing. She especially likes learning new things and spend much of her time practicing he cursive handwriting.

Xiomara loves fashion, clothes, and jewelry. She also enjoys music and dancing. Xiomara's favorite animal is the cat.

24